KW-051-855

HEINEMANN GUIDED READERS
INTERMEDIATE LEVEL

DICK FRANCIS

Banker

Retold by Stephen Colbourn

LIVERPOOL HOPE
UNIVERSITY COLLEGE

LIBRARY

PO BOX 95
LIVERPOOL L16 9LB

HEINEMANN

INTERMEDIATE LEVEL

Series Editor: John Milne

The Heinemann Guided Readers provide a choice of enjoyable reading material for learners of English. The series is published at five levels – Starter, Beginner, Elementary, Intermediate and Upper. At **Intermediate Level**, the control of content and language has the following main features:

Information Control
Information which is vital to the understanding of the story is presented in an easily assimilated manner and is repeated when necessary. Difficult allusion and metaphor are avoided and cultural backgrounds are made explicit.

Structure Control
Most of the structures used in the Readers will be familiar to students who have completed an elementary course of English. Other grammatical features may occur, but their use is made clear through context and reinforcement. This ensures that the reading, as well as being enjoyable, provides a continual learning situation for the students. Sentences are limited in most cases to a maximum of three clauses and within sentences there is a balanced use of adverbial and adjectival phrases. Great care is taken with pronoun reference.

Vocabulary Control
There is a basic vocabulary of approximately 1,600 words. Help is given to the students in the form of illustrations, which are closely related to the text.

Glossary
Some difficult words and phrases in this book are important for understanding the story. Some of these words are explained in the story, some are shown in the pictures, and others are marked with a number like this . . .[3] Words with a number are explained in the Glossary on page 73.

Contents

The People in This Story

Tim (Timothy) Ekaterin

Gordon Michaels

Judith Michaels

Dissdale Smith

Calder Jackson

Henry Shipton

Ursula Young

Oliver Knowles

Ginnie Knowles

Ian Pargetter

Pen Warner

Ricky Barnet

5

1

The First Year: May

Paul Ekaterin Limited is the name of a bank. Ee-*ka*-te-rin sounds a strange name. But it is my own name. I am Timothy Ekaterin, great-grandson of Paul Ekaterin, who started the bank many years ago.

I work for the bank. Now, I know what you will think. You will think I am the son of rich parents. You will think I have a good job in the family bank. You will think I do very little work and earn[1] a lot of money. Most people think that. But it is *not* true.

All these things were true of my father. He was very rich. He never worked. He spent all his money on parties . . . on travel . . . on fine clothes and on champagne. He was a kind man, but not very clever. He died of drink[2].

My mother was a gambler[3]. She gambled on horses and lost, again and again. When my father died, there was no money left.

My uncle helped us. Uncle Freddie owns the bank – Paul Ekaterin Limited. He gave money to my mother, but made her promise not to gamble. And he gave me a job.

I did not want to be a banker, but I had no money and I needed a job. Very soon, I liked working in the bank. The work was interesting and I was good at it.

But Uncle Freddie was not sure about me. He was afraid that I would drink and gamble like my parents. But I worked harder than anyone else in the bank. I wanted to be successful.

Paul Ekaterin Limited is a merchant bank. A merchant

bank lends money to people in business. The borrowers pay interest on the loans. The bank's profit comes from the interest paid by the borrowers.

Lending money is like gambling. It's a risk. You can win or you can lose. But if the bank does not lend money, it does not make any interest. No interest . . . no profit.

Many people come to the bank wanting to borrow money. I work in the department that decides whether to lend them money or not. We say 'yes' or 'no'. We want to be sure that we will get our money back. Sometimes, we are not sure. If we say 'yes', we take a risk. We may lose the money.

My boss, Gordon Michaels, always made the important decisions in our department. One morning, he was late for work. I wondered where he was.

Gordon came to the bank, but he did not go inside. He went to the fountain outside the building and walked into the water!

Gordon stood in the fountain. He was wearing an expensive, black suit . . . a white shirt . . . expensive, black shoes. Water was running down over his hair . . . his face . . . his expensive clothes. Gordon was an important banker. Important bankers do not stand in fountains, getting wet.

People were looking out of the windows of the building. They did not understand what was happening. I ran downstairs and spoke to Gordon quietly. At first, he did not understand me. Then he let me help him out of the fountain. The chairman of the bank[4], Henry Shipton, took Gordon into his office.

An hour later, I was sitting at my desk. The phone rang. It was Henry Shipton.

Gordon stood in the fountain. Water was running down
over his hair . . .

'Can you come up to my office, Tim?' the chairman asked.

I went upstairs to the chairman's office. A secretary opened the door for me. Henry was sitting at his large desk.

'Come in, Tim,' the chairman said. 'I'm afraid that Gordon is ill.'

'What's the matter with him?' I asked.

'I have spoken to his wife, Judith, on the phone,' Henry said. 'It's his heart. Gordon has a weak heart and has to take pills. Last week, Gordon's doctor gave him some new pills. Well, these new pills have made Gordon very ill. He doesn't know what he's doing. He needs a long rest and I've sent him home in my car.'

'And who will look after the department while he's away?' I asked.

'Well, Tim,' Henry said. 'Gordon thinks that you're very good at your job. I want you to look after the department while he's away.'

'Thank you,' I said. I was very pleased.

The chairman smiled. 'If you need any advice, ask the people in your department,' he said. 'Come to me if you need any help.'

'Yes, I will,' I said. Then I went back to my desk. I was very happy. I was thirty-two years old and this was my first really important job. But it was not an easy job. I was afraid of making mistakes. I was afraid of taking risks. I was afraid of losing the bank's money.

I studied the files[5]. There were several requests for loans[6] in the files. One of them was a request from an artist who wanted to make cartoon films[7]. This looked like a big risk. But, I thought, the artist may become famous like Walt Disney.

Walt Disney made the Mickey Mouse cartoons and they made millions of dollars. So I asked the artist to come and see me at the office.

Another request was from a company in South America. I asked my colleagues in the department about this request. The Research Department had studied the request earlier. They had written a report about it. I read their report for the rest of the day.

It is much easier to say 'no' than to say 'yes'. But, if the bank always says 'no', then the bank does not make any money.

In the end, I wrote a very polite letter to the South American company, saying 'no'. I hoped I was right.

2

The First Year: June

After three weeks, Gordon phoned me. He was feeling much better.

'Judith and I want to thank you for helping me,' he said. 'I've got tickets for the races at Ascot[8] next week. Will you come as our guest?'

'I'd love to come,' I said, 'but I have to work. I can't take a day off.'

'Yes, you can,' Gordon said, with a laugh. 'The chairman's coming as well. Henry says you've been working very hard. He says you can have the day off.'

I wanted to go to the races at Ascot very much. I wanted to meet Judith Michaels again.

'If the chairman says it's OK, I'll come,' I said.

——

I spent three hours with the artist who wanted to make cartoon films. The young man wanted a lot of money from the bank. I was not sure. It was a risk. I took some of the artist's drawings to the chairman.

'How old is this artist?' Henry asked.

'Twenty-four,' I said.

Henry shook his head. 'And how much money does he want to borrow?'

'He wants a hundred thousand pounds,' I said.

'That much!' Henry said. 'Why haven't you said "no"?'

'Because of these,' I said, putting the artist's drawings on the table in front of him.

The chairman was not a man who smiled very often. But as he looked through the drawings, he began to laugh. I still expected him to say 'no', but all he said was – 'It's your decision.'

I decided to gamble and say 'yes'.

——

Royal Ascot is one of the most important race meetings of the year. Women wear expensive clothes and beautiful hats. Men wear expensive suits and top hats[9].

Gordon welcomed me to his box[10]. He gave me a glass of champagne.

'Let me introduce you to everyone,' Gordon said. 'You know my wife, Judith, of course. And over here is Mr Dissdale Smith and his wife, Bettina. Dissdale – Bettina – this is Tim Ekaterin.'

I shook hands with everyone in the box. Everyone was drinking champagne and laughing and talking. They talked about the horses they were going to bet on[11].

At the back of the box, there was a large table. An excellent lunch was laid out on the table.

I sat down next to Judith, Gordon's wife. She was much younger than Gordon. She was about my age. She had dark brown hair and large, blue eyes. She was wearing a bright yellow silk dress and a hat decorated with flowers. She looked very beautiful. I was happy to be sitting beside her.

I was not married. I wished I had met Judith before she married Gordon. I had loved her from the moment I saw her.

'Here comes our important guest,' Judith said. 'Calder Jackson.'

'Who?' I asked.

'Calder Jackson – the man who cures[12] sick horses,' Judith replied.

Calder Jackson was a short man with a lot of grey, curly hair. He had a small beard around his chin. I listened to him talking to one of the ladies.

'I'm not a vet[13] or a doctor,' he was saying. 'But sick horses get better when I look after them. I touch them and they are cured.'

'Really?' I said. I did not believe him. 'Do all your sick horses always get better?'

'Sadly, no,' Calder Jackson said. 'Not all.'

He smiled, showing perfect, white teeth. He was a good-looking man. The ladies all smiled back at him.

As we ate lunch, we talked about the horses which were running in the races.

'Which horse should we bet on in the next race?' Gordon asked Calder Jackson.

'I'm going to bet on Sandcastle. He's the best horse here, today. He's sure to win,' Calder Jackson said.

The others went off to put a bet on Sandcastle. I did not want to gamble, so I stayed in the box with Dissdale Smith. Dissdale was looking pale. I wondered if he had eaten and drunk too much.

'Are you going to bet?' I asked.

'I've bet on Sandcastle already,' Dissdale replied. 'In fact, I've put *all* my money on the horse. Everything!'

I said nothing. I thought of my mother. She had lost all my father's money on horses.

The others came back to the box. The race started. Eight horses raced round the track[14]. Sandcastle was not at the front. Sandcastle stayed in fourth or fifth place. Dissdale Smith looked pale and ill. He sat down on a chair at the back of the box.

'Sandcastle is moving ahead . . .' shouted the commentator[15], '. . . he's in third place.'

As the horses ran towards the finishing line, Sandcastle was in second place. Then he was running beside the first horse!

'Look!' I shouted to Dissdale, 'your horse is going to win!' We all stood up. The crowd was shouting with excitement.

Sandcastle crossed the finishing line first. He had won!

13

'Look! Your horse is going to win!'

Dissdale sat down again, looking very ill.

'I've won,' Dissdale said. 'I'll never put *all* my money on one horse ever again!'

Everyone, except me, had bet on Sandcastle. The others had all won money. They thanked Calder Jackson.

At the end of the afternoon, we all left the races together. Calder Jackson was talking to the ladies. All the ladies laughed at Calder Jackson's jokes.

I saw a boy watching us. He was looking at Calder Jackson strangely.

The boy, who was wearing jeans, was about sixteen years old. Suddenly, he pulled out a knife and ran straight at Calder Jackson.

The knife was pointing at Calder Jackson's stomach. I jumped and hit the boy's arm. The boy dropped the knife and we both fell over.

I held the boy until strong arms pulled me back. Two policemen had taken hold of me. I let go of the boy. He got up and ran into the crowd.

The police thought that I had attacked the boy. They thought it was my fault.

'What do you think that knife is doing there?' I asked, pointing to the knife on the ground. 'That boy tried to kill Calder Jackson. I stopped him.'

I was taken to the police station. The police asked me a lot of questions.

'No, I don't know who the boy was,' I said. 'No, I've never seen him before in my life.'

They let me go and I left the police station with Calder Jackson. There were newspaper reporters[16] outside.

They took photographs and wanted to ask me questions.

Suddenly, he pulled out a knife and ran straight at Calder Jackson.

I did not want to speak to them. I wanted to go home. Gordon and Judith Michaels were waiting for me. They took me back to my flat in their car. My photograph appeared in the newspapers the next day. Beneath the photograph were the words: 'The man who saved the life of the famous Calder Jackson'.

3

The First Year: October

Gordon was well again. He came back to the office and I went back to my old job.

I was worried about the money I had lent to the cartoon artist. I spoke to Gordon about the loan.

'It's a lot of money to risk on one man,' Gordon said. 'You know, before my . . . illness . . .' Gordon did not like to speak about the day he had walked into the fountain. '. . . I was going to say "no" to this man. How is his work going?'

'Fine,' I said. 'He's nearly finished his first short film.'

The phone rang. It was the artist. I had spoken too soon.

'I've hired[17] three more men,' the artist said, 'and I need five more men. I need to increase my loan[18].'

'Wait!' I said 'You can't have any more money!'

'But I've bought a new studio[19],' the artist continued. 'I've said that Ekaterin Bank will lend me the money.'

'You can't do that,' I said. 'You can't continue to borrow money!'

I was very worried. My heart was beating quickly. I had lent the man over a hundred thousand pounds of the bank's money. He had spent it all and now he wanted more! I thought of the bank losing all that money. I would lose my job after this!

'Listen,' the artist said, 'I've sold my first film to BBC Television. They want more of my films. And a film company wants to buy some of my films, too. I've signed a contract for twenty films!'

My heart slowed down. 'Come over to the bank with the contracts,' I said. 'We'll arrange the extra loan.'

'Oh, thank you, that's wonderful,' the artist said. 'I thought it would be all right. I mean, once we've finished all these films, I can pay back the loan easily.'

I put the phone down, feeling weak.

'Is there a problem?' Gordon asked.

'No,' I said with relief[20]. 'That was the cartoon artist on the phone. I've bet on a winner!'

We heard that Uncle Freddie was in the building. My Uncle Freddie, as I said earlier, owned the bank. Everyone looked busy as he came round each department. Although he had retired[21], Uncle Freddie still liked to visit the bank.

I received a message to go up to the chairman's office. I went upstairs and found Uncle Freddie and Henry Shipton waiting for me.

'Congratulations!' Uncle Freddie said to me. 'You're now a director[22] of Paul Ekaterin Limited.'

'Pardon?' I said. 'A what?'

'A director,' my uncle said. 'You know – a man who sits on the bank's Board of Directors.'

'But, do you think I'm ready for the job?' I asked.

'Don't you want to be a director?' my uncle asked.

'Yes, I do,' I replied.

'Good, then that's settled,' he said.

'All the directors agree,' said Henry. 'We discussed it at our meeting, this morning. It's time another Ekaterin took his place on the Board of Directors.'

The next week, I had lunch with all the directors. They welcomed me to the Board. At the age of thirty-two, I was the youngest director in the history of the bank.

4

The First Year: November

The chairman asked me to look at an unusual request for a loan. A horse-breeder[23] had asked for a loan to buy a racehorse.

'It's Sandcastle,' Henry told me, as we were eating lunch in the directors' dining-room. 'You remember our day at Ascot? He's the horse we all bet on.'

'Who wants to buy him?' I asked.

'A horse-breeder called Oliver Knowles,' the chairman said. 'He wants to use the horse to breed champion racehorses.'

'How much does he want to borrow?' I asked.

'Five million pounds,' Henry said. 'It's a lot of money. The bank has never risked money on a racehorse before. Will you look into it[24] for us?'

'Yes,' I said, 'I will.'

First, I arranged a meeting with an expert on horse-breeding. She was called Ursula Young. I asked her to tell me everything about horse-breeding.

'You expect a champion racehorse stallion to breed champion racehorses,' Ursula Young said. 'After the stallion has been with the mare, you have to wait eleven months before a foal is born. Then you have to wait for two years. Young horses don't race until they're two years old. So you don't know for three years if your champion is breeding champions.'

'I see,' I said. 'And how soon does a horse-breeder expect to make a profit on a stallion?'

'After three years,' Ursula said.

'So, a horse-breeder makes a clear profit after three years?' I said.

'Yes,' Ursula said, 'and a good breeding stallion can go on making money for ten or fifteen years. It's a very profitable business.'

I thanked Ursula Young and went back to the bank. I worked out the details[25] on a loan of five million pounds. Then I phoned Oliver Knowles – the man who wanted to buy Sandcastle. I arranged to visit him at the weekend.

On Sunday, I drove to Oliver Knowles' stables in Hertfordshire. The stables were about sixty-four kilometres north of London. Oliver Knowles was a neat and tidy man. He lived in a neat and tidy house. All around the stables, there were green fields and white fences.

Oliver Knowles welcomed me. 'Mr Ekaterin,' he said, 'I'm very pleased to meet you. Please come and look round the stables.'

He showed me round the stables. His dog followed us.

Three brown heads appeared over three stable doors. These were the heads of three stallions.

'This one is Rotaboy,' Oliver Knowles said. He gave the horse a carrot. 'Rotaboy is twenty years old. Next to him is Diarist – he's nearly sixteen. The last one is Parakeet. He'll be twelve in January.'

Oliver Knowles gave a carrot to each of the horses. 'They're getting old,' he said. 'That's why I need a new, young stallion. If I can buy Sandcastle, I can make these stables world famous.'

We went into the house. Oliver Knowles had already worked out the details of a five million pound loan. He showed me some figures and said, 'If the bank will lend me the money, I can pay it back in five years.'

'You will have to pay us interest on the loan,' I said. 'the total will be nearly eight million pounds. Can you make eight million pounds in five years?'

'I'm sure I can,' said Oliver Knowles.

At that moment, a girl came into the room with some tea.

'This is my daughter, Ginnie,' Oliver Knowles said. 'My wife isn't here at the moment.'

We drank tea and I studied Oliver Knowles' figures. 'I'll take these back to the bank,' I said. 'Five million pounds is a lot of money. The chairman of the bank must make the final decision. And he won't do that until we have made a complete check. However, if everything is in order, I think the bank will lend you the money.'

'Thank you,' he said. We shook hands.

Ginnie came back into the room. She was now wearing school uniform. 'You won't forget that I have to go back to school this afternoon, will you, Dad?' she said.

Oliver Knowles gave a carrot to each of the horses.

'Oh well, perhaps in half an hour,' Oliver Knowles said. Then he turned to me.

'Are you going in the direction of High Wycombe?' he asked. 'Her mother usually takes her back to school. But, as I said, my wife is away at the moment. I may as well tell you – she isn't coming back.'

'I'd be pleased to take Ginnie back to school,' I said.

I drove Ginnie to her boarding school. She talked happily, until she spoke about her mother.

'Everything's changed since Mum went away.'

Ginnie was silent for a moment. 'I'm sure you don't want to hear about it.'

I stopped outside the school. Ginnie got out of the car, gave me a quick smile and said, 'Thanks for the lift[26].'

I felt sorry for Ginnie. Her mother had left home and her father was busy all the time. I hoped her father would be successful – both for him and for me. Five million pounds was a lot of money to lose on a horse.

5

The First Year: December

I made a report to the Board of Directors. I told them of my meetings with Ursula Young and Oliver Knowles. They decided that Sandcastle was a good risk, so the bank lent five million pounds to Oliver Knowles. It was such an unusual loan, that it was reported in a number of newspapers.

Henry Shipton called me to his office.

'Tim,' he said, 'I'd like you to visit Mr Knowles from time to time. I want you to make sure everything is all right at the stables. I want you to look after our five million pounds.'

——

I received two invitations that day. Gordon asked – 'Have you made any plans for Christmas?'

'No, I haven't,' I said.

'Well, Judith and I wondered if you'd like to stay with us for a few days at Christmas.'

I had not seen Judith since the day at Ascot. I remembered how lovely she had looked in her yellow dress. I wanted to say 'yes'. I wanted to see her again. But was it right? I felt very strongly about her. I thought quickly. If the invitation was from Judith and Gordon, then Judith wanted me to come.

'I'd love to come,' I said, 'very much.'

A second invitation came from Calder Jackson. I was invited for lunch at his stables in Newmarket[27], on the following Sunday. I accepted this invitation also.

I drove to Newmarket on Sunday. Calder Jackson showed me the horses in his stables.

'Some of these horses were very sick when they came here,' Calder said. 'Look at them now. They're all strong and healthy.'

'But how do you cure these horses?' I asked. 'Do you give them any special drugs or medicines?'

'Come and see my drug store[28],' Calder Jackson replied.

He led me to a door marked "Surgery". We went inside.

There were many shelves on the walls. The shelves were covered with bottles and boxes and the room had a sweet smell.

'These are all natural drugs and medicines,' Calder said. He pointed to the bottles and boxes. 'All my medicines are herbal. They come from plants. I never use chemicals or artificial drugs.'

During lunch, Calder talked about herbs and the illnesses they cure. He knew all the names of the herbs and which illnesses they cured. He also spoke about his fees[29]. Calder Jackson's horse hospital was expensive – very expensive. His business had made him a rich man.

There were two other guests for lunch. I had met one of them before – Dissdale Smith. He was the man who had put all his money on Sandcastle at Ascot. The other guest was a vet called Ian Pargetter.

'What do you think of Calder's unusual medicines?' I asked him.

'Calder has succeeded where vets have failed,' Ian Pargetter said. 'I have seen him cure very sick horses. Very sick horses come here. In a week or two, they have left here strong and healthy again. His medicines are unusual, but they are successful.'

Later, I remembered that Sunday lunch. It was the last time I saw Ian Pargetter alive.

We had a good time at Christmas. Judith and Gordon Michaels made me feel very comfortable in their home.

Judith had invited another guest, Pen Warner, who lived nearby. Pen Warner was a pharmacist[30]. I told her about

There were two other guests – Dissdale Smith and Ian Pargetter.

Calder Jackson's natural herbal medicines for horses.

'What do you think about herbal medicines?' I asked.

'It is well-known that many herbs can cure illnesses,' Pen Warner said. 'I've seen Calder Jackson on television. He says he can cure horses by touching them. I don't know if this is true. But many people seem to believe him.'

It was difficult for me to stay in the same house with Gordon's wife, Judith. She knew that I often looked at her. I was sure that she understood my thoughts. But – she was Gordon's wife.

I went back to my lonely flat on the day after Christmas.

6

The Second Year: February

On 1st February, I phoned Calder Jackson. I wanted to invite him to dinner.

'Look, Tim,' Calder said, 'I can't talk to you now. Something terrible has happened.'

'What's the matter?' I asked.

'Ian Pargetter, the vet, has been murdered,' Calder said. 'He often helped me with sick horses. But I don't think you knew him.'

'Yes, I did,' I said. 'I met him at your house before Christmas.'

'Did you? Oh, yes,' Calder said. 'I'm very upset. I can't think. Look, Tim, can you phone me some other time?'

'Yes, of course,' I said and put the phone down.

Next day, the newspapers reported the murder. Ian Pargetter's wife and daughter had been away. Ian Pargetter had been working until late in the evening. When he returned home, he had found a burglar in his house. The burglar had hit him on the head and killed him. Nothing was stolen from the house except the vet's medicine case. The case had contained a few drugs for animals.

———

Two weeks later, I visited Oliver Knowles again. The stables were busy. Many men were working – exercising the horses, cleaning the stables and carrying food and water for the horses.

Oliver Knowles showed me his five million pound prize. Sandcastle was looking over the door of his stable. Oliver gave the horse a carrot.

'Jason!' Oliver Knowles shouted to one of the stable lads.

'Yes, sir?' Jason called back.

'Take Sandcastle down to the small field for some exercise,' Oliver Knowles said.

Jason fixed a rope to Sandcastle's headcollar[31].

'We'll go and watch Sandcastle exercising,' Oliver Knowles said to me. So we walked towards the small field.

It was Sunday. I thought of Oliver Knowles' daughter, Ginnie – the girl I had taken back to school in November.

'Does your daughter still come home at weekends?' I asked.

'Yes, she is here today. She comes home from school every

weekend,' Oliver said. 'She helps around the stables. She likes working with horses.'

As we were walking along, Oliver stopped to feed carrots to his old stallions. Suddenly, we heard a cry and the sound of a horse running. We both turned round in surprise.

'Sandcastle!' Oliver Knowles shouted and started to run.

I ran after him. We found Jason on the ground. Another stable lad was helping him up. Jason had been opening a gate and Sandcastle had pulled the rope from his hands and had run away.

'After him!' Oliver shouted. 'Get the Land Rover! We mustn't let Sandcastle reach the road!'

They all ran towards the garage. I was left alone. I did not know what to do. The horse had disappeared behind a hedge. I started to run after it.

Ginnie had heard the noise. She came running towards me from the house.

'This way!' I shouted and we both ran round the hedge towards the road.

We reached the road and looked both ways. There was no sign[32] of Sandcastle.

A car came past. It was travelling at about ninety kilometres an hour – too fast to stop quickly.

'If Sandcastle's on the road, he'll be killed by a car,' Ginnie said, almost in tears.

I thought of the bank and my job. It was frightening. A five million pound traffic accident was waiting to happen!

'Dad will be coming along the road,' said Ginnie.

'There's a lane on the other side of the road. We'll look there.'

We ran across the road and down the lane. It was very

muddy. I almost fell over and my trousers were covered with mud.

There were high hedges on either side of the narrow lane. Then the lane opened into a wider space. There stood Sandcastle, his head high, his nose in the wind.

Ginnie stopped running and caught my arm.

'Don't move,' she said. 'Don't frighten him.'

I stood still, while Ginnie moved forward slowly. She held out her left hand, pretending to offer[33] the horse a carrot. She slowly moved her right hand towards the rope which hung from the horse's headcollar.

Sandcastle turned suddenly, knocking her over, and ran past me. Without thinking, I caught the rope that hung from his headcollar and held tight.

Sandcastle was very strong. I was pulled off my feet and the horse kicked my legs. But I held on to the rope, pulling Sandcastle's head down. The horse stopped running, after a few metres. I was covered with mud. My legs were cut and my hands were bleeding.

Ginnie ran up to me. She was crying.

'You – you could have been killed,' she said.

'It doesn't matter now,' I said. 'I'm all right. Get your father. I can't hold this horse much longer.'

Oliver Knowles arrived in the Land Rover with the two stable lads.

'Don't ever, *ever* try to catch hold of a running horse,' he said angrily. 'You can get killed!'

'So Ginnie told me,' I said, as I handed Sandcastle over to his owner.

'Never do it again,' said Oliver Knowles. Then he smiled with relief. 'And thanks. Thanks for looking after my horse.'

Without thinking, I caught the rope that hung from his headcollar and held tight.

7

The Second Year: April

When Calder Jackson came to London, I invited him to dinner at a famous restaurant. Everyone in the restaurant knew Calder Jackson's face. They had seen him on television. People stared at us and listened to our conversation.

I felt embarrassed[34], but Calder was happy. He liked an audience. He talked loudly, so that everyone could hear what he said. He talked about his recent visit to America. He talked about his herbal medicines. I said very little.

Before he left the restaurant, Calder said to me, 'Come to my stables at Newmarket again. You're always welcome.'

So, I decided to visit him again.

———

I was very busy at the bank. There was a lot of work to do in the office. Also, Gordon was not well and I helped him as much as I could. He was often tired and pale.

I thought about Judith, Gordon's wife. The last time I had seen her was at Christmas. Now, it was nearly the Easter holiday. I wanted to see her. So one morning, I spoke to Gordon.

'Gordon,' I said, 'would you like to go out somewhere on Easter Monday? I'd like to take you and Judith out for the day. Perhaps Pen Warner, who I met at Christmas, would like to come too?'

'That sounds a good idea,' Gordon said. 'Where shall we go?'

'That,' I said, 'will be a surprise.'

On Easter Monday, I drove to Clapham, where Gordon lived. Gordon, Judith and Pen were waiting for me. The ladies were excited. Gordon did not look well.

'Do you mind if I sit in the back of the car and sleep a little?' Gordon asked. 'I'm feeling very tired today.'

I drove towards Cambridge. I had phoned Calder Jackson earlier in the week. I had arranged a visit to Calder Jackson's stables at Newmarket.

'Where are we going?' Judith asked.

'We are going to see Calder Jackson,' I replied.

'How interesting!' said Pen. 'Don't tell him I'm a pharmacist. I'd like to hear what he says about his herbal medicines.'

So we promised not to tell Calder what Pen's job was.

Calder was expecting us and came out of his house to welcome us.

'Come in. Come in and have some coffee,' he said. 'Then I'll show you round the stables.'

He showed us all the stables. We saw the horses which he had cured.

'Now, come and see my drug store,' Calder said.

He led us to the door marked "Surgery". The last time I had been here was before Ian Pargetter, the vet, was murdered.

Calder talked and talked. He told us all about his herbal medicines.

'I make the pills for the horses myself,' he said, and showed us a machine for making pills.

Pen looked around the surgery with interest. She saw a pill

We looked around Calder Jackson's surgery.

that had fallen on the floor. She picked it up and put it on the table. We all saw it.

We came out of the surgery, and Calder said, 'Come into the house for a drink.'

But Gordon was cold and tired. It was time for us to go. We thanked Calder, got in the car and drove away.

Pen said, 'He doesn't make all his own pills. And not all his medicines are made from herbs.'

'What did you find?' I asked.

'You saw me pick up that pill,' Pen said. 'Well, it was warfarin[35]. Warfarin is a drug that doctors give to people who've had heart attacks.'

'Can you buy warfarin pills in a chemist's shop?' I asked.

'No, you have to get them from a doctor or a vet,' Pen said.

After lunch in a country hotel, we drove to Oliver Knowles' stables. I wanted to show Sandcastle to the others.

Ginnie, Oliver Knowles' daughter, showed us round the stables and the fields. We saw the mares and their young foals. And we saw the famous Sandcastle.

'Did you tell people about how Sandcastle ran away?' asked Ginnie.

'No, I didn't,' I said. 'I didn't want the bank to know about that. I didn't want anyone to know that our five million pound horse nearly got killed on the road.'

'It won't happen again,' said Ginnie. 'We've had new fences built all round the stables and new locks put on all the stable doors.'

It was late in the afternoon. We said goodbye to Ginnie and drove to London. It had been a good day. We were all very happy.

I took Gordon, Judith and Pen back to Clapham. Gordon

After lunch we drove to Oliver Knowles' stables.

was very tired and I could see he wanted to go to bed.

Judith came out to the car to say goodbye to me. It was dark. We stood for a moment in silence. I held her in my arms.

'It's been a lovely day,' she said.

I kissed her quickly, got in the car and drove away.

8

The Second Year: October

Summer was cold and wet that year, but in the autumn, the weather was much better. I went to the races at Newbury on a bright Saturday afternoon in October.

I saw Ursula Young. She was the woman who had told me all about horse-breeding. We had a drink together in the bar.

'I was in Newmarket last week,' Ursula Young said. 'I met Ian Pargetter's wife, poor thing. I felt so sorry for her when her husband was murdered.'

'The police never caught the murderer, did they?' I asked.

'No,' Ursula replied. 'They say they're still looking. But Ian was murdered nine months ago. I don't think they'll find the murderer now.'

Then Ursula looked at her watch. 'Oh, someone is waiting for me. I must go.'

We left the bar and immediately a small man came up to us.

'There you are! I've been looking everywhere for you,' he said to Ursula.

'You're a little early, Fred,' Ursula Young said. She introduced me to the small man.

'This is Fred Barnet. And this is his wife, Susan – and his son, Ricky.'

I shook hands with them all, saying – 'Pleased to meet you. My name's Tim Ekaterin.'

When I said my name, the son, Ricky, went pale and his eyes opened wide. He looked very frightened. I knew him at once. He was the boy who had tried to kill Calder Jackson with a knife!

Mr and Mrs Barnet were busy talking to Ursula Young. I walked a few steps away with Ricky.

'I should call the police straightaway,' I said quietly. 'Perhaps I will. But, first, tell me why you tried to kill Calder Jackson.'

Ricky was very frightened. 'Don't tell my mum and dad,' he said. 'They don't know anything.'

He seemed more afraid that I would tell his parents than the police. 'How old are you?' I asked.

'Seventeen,' the boy said.

'Tell me what happened,' I said.

'It was because of a horse,' he began, 'a horse called Indian Silk.'

'Indian Silk?' I asked. 'Isn't that the horse which won the Gold Cup at Cheltenham in March?'

'That's the one,' said Ricky. 'My dad owned that horse until two years ago. Indian Silk won here at Newbury and we were going to race him at Ascot. My dad thought Indian Silk was a champion. But the horse got sick – really ill – and we thought it was going to die.'

Ricky looked at the ground. 'Well,' he continued, 'my dad

39

'. . . tell me why you tried to kill Calder Jackson.'

was really upset and my mum was crying. And I'd got exams at school and couldn't study. The vets couldn't help the poor horse. Everything was going wrong.'

'So, who did cure the horse?' I asked.

'Well, a man phoned my dad and said he'd buy the horse.'

'Buy a dying horse? What for?' I asked.

'The man said he'd keep it and look after it,' Ricky said. 'He said that the horse would never race again. He said he would keep it in a field. He offered to pay Dad a few hundred pounds, so Dad sold the horse.'

'What happened after the man bought Indian Silk?' I asked.

'He stayed in a field for a few weeks,' Ricky said. 'Then he was taken to Calder Jackson's place.'

'And Calder Jackson cured him?'

'Well,' Ricky said, 'the horse got better so quickly, my dad thought it had never been sick at all. He was very angry. He called Calder Jackson a thief! My mum was in tears. I failed my exams. I didn't know what I was doing. I took a kitchen knife and went to Ascot and waited for Calder Jackson. I'd seen him on TV, so I knew what he looked like. Well . . . you know the rest . . . and I'm glad you stopped me. If I'd killed him, I'd be in prison.'

'Tell me,' I said, 'who bought the horse from your father?'

'A man called Dissdale Smith,' Ricky said. 'Do you know him?'

'Yes, I know Mr Dissdale Smith,' I said. 'He was standing beside me and Calder Jackson that day at Ascot.'

Ricky looked very sad. I was not sure what to do. Was Ricky dangerous? Would he try to kill someone else?

41

I made a decision. I did not think that the boy was really dangerous. 'I won't tell anyone,' I said.

Ricky was surprised. He did not believe me.

'You won't tell anyone?' he asked, looking at my face.

I nodded. 'You'd better go and find your parents,' I said.

Ricky turned and walked happily away. I watched him go. I hoped I had done the right thing.

9

The Second Year: November

I had seen Judith only twice since Easter. I had seen her at a party and, once, at the bank. We had not had much time to talk to each other.

Gordon invited me to his house in Clapham again.

'Come for lunch on Sunday,' he said. 'This year, Judith and I are going to Edinburgh for Christmas. We'd like you to visit us before we go.'

I went to Clapham on Sunday. Pen Warner, the pharmacist, was there as well.

We were eating lunch when I said, 'I saw the boy who tried to kill Calder Jackson.'

Gordon was surprised. 'You've told the police, haven't you?' he asked.

'No,' I replied. I told them about Ricky Barnet and the horse, Indian Silk, and about Dissdale Smith and Calder Jackson. I told them how Dissdale Smith had bought the dying horse and that Calder Jackson had cured it.

'Dissdale is a gambler,' Pen said. 'I suppose he made a big profit when he resold the horse.'

'It was a very big risk,' Judith said. 'But, remember, he gambled all his money on Sandcastle at Ascot. He won! He's lucky.'

He was lucky, certainly. But his gamble on Indian Silk made me suspicious[36]. Was it only luck? Or was there another reason?

———

I went to Oliver Knowles' stables at the end of November. He had been very busy. Now, nearly all of the stables and fields were empty. The mares and foals had gone home. The farm was quiet in the winter months.

Ginnie showed me around, as usual. She talked about all the mares which had been to the stables.

'We expect about forty foals to be born in the spring,' she said.

'You seem to be very happy,' I said. 'You like working with your father, don't you?'

'Yes,' Ginnie smiled. 'I'll leave school next year. Then I'm going to work here all the time. I'll be Dad's assistant. I love working with horses.'

I was pleased that she was happy. She and her father had worked very hard. I hoped they would be successful.

10

The Third Year: April

The trouble started with a phone call. Oliver Knowles phoned me at the office on a Thursday morning.

'Tim,' he said, 'can you come to the stables immediately?'

'What's wrong?' I asked. 'Is it Sandcastle?' I suddenly felt very worried.

'I'll tell you when you come,' Oliver Knowles said. 'It's very urgent!'

'I'll come at once,' I said, and put the phone down. Before leaving the office, I told Gordon where I was going.

'Don't worry too much,' Gordon said. 'The horse is insured[37] against everything. Oliver Knowles is paying thousands of pounds to insure the horse. If the horse has an accident . . . is sick . . . if it dies . . . the insurance company will pay for it.'

I drove to Oliver Knowles' stables as fast as I could. Oliver was waiting for me.

'What's the matter with Sandcastle?' I asked.

'Sandcastle isn't ill,' Oliver said. 'Come inside and I'll show you.'

We went into the sitting-room. Oliver showed me three letters.

'These are from horse owners who sent their mares here to breed from Sandcastle. Their mares have given birth to Sandcastle's foals. Read the letters,' he said.

I read the letters. Three foals had been born. All three foals had been deformed[38]. One foal had only half a foot. Another

44

had only one ear. The third had died as soon as it was born.

'I've also had two phone calls,' Oliver said. 'Two more foals died as soon as they were born. They were badly deformed. Sandcastle is breeding deformed foals. I'm ruined[39]!'

'Not yet,' I said. 'Let me look at the insurance policy. If there is something wrong with Sandcastle, the insurance company will pay.'

Oliver showed me the insurance policy, then went into the kitchen to make coffee. I read the insurance policy. It was very long. The horse was insured against almost everything – fire, flood, accident, poisoning[40]. It was insured against being unable to breed. But there was nothing in the policy about breeding deformed foals.

Oliver brought coffee. 'It's bad, isn't it?' he said.

I said nothing. I was very worried. If Sandcastle's foals were deformed, Oliver Knowles would lose his business. No one would send their mares to the stables to breed. Oliver Knowles needed five good years of business to pay back his loan to the bank. Now, after only one year, Oliver Knowles was ruined.

If Oliver Knowles could not pay back the money, the bank would lose five million pounds. The bank had gambled on a horse and lost. But Oliver Knowles had lost everything – his business, his house, all his property – everything! He was ruined.

'Don't tell anyone, yet,' I said. 'We must have the horse tested by vets[41]. We must find out if there is a problem with the horse itself. We must find out why these foals are deformed.'

'But what could be the problem?' Oliver asked. 'I look after all my horses very carefully.'

'I don't know,' I said. 'Perhaps it's poison. It could be something in the food or water.'

Ginnie came in. She looked at our faces.

'What's wrong?' she asked. 'What's the matter?'

'Nothing,' Oliver said.

'Don't tell me that! I'm not a child,' Ginnie said. 'Something terrible has happened, hasn't it?'

Oliver looked at her sadly. 'You'll have to know sometime,' he said. 'Some of Sandcastle's foals aren't . . . perfect.'

'What do you mean, not perfect?' Ginnie wanted to know.

Oliver told her about the deformed foals. 'And if there are more deformed foals, we can't allow Sandcastle to breed. I'll have to return everyone's money – or as much as I can.'

When I left them, Ginnie was crying.

The next morning, I had to tell the chairman and the Board of Directors. I had recommended[42] the loan to Oliver Knowles. It had been my decision to lend the money.

One of the directors was very angry – 'FIVE . . . MILLION . . . POUNDS!' he said slowly and loudly. 'Do you understand how much five million pounds is worth? And you've lost it on a horse!'

'Tim,' the chairman said to me, 'go back to Oliver Knowles' stables. Look at his accounts[43]. Find out how much money we've lost exactly – if we've lost it. We can't be sure, yet.'

I drove to Oliver Knowles' stables. Oliver was pleased to see me and asked me to stay.

'Stay for the weekend, if you like,' he said. 'There's more bad news, I'm afraid. Another deformed foal has been born. This one had no front feet. The poor thing had to be destroyed[44].'

Ginnie could not stop crying. 'Dad's ruined, isn't he?' she said. 'He can't pay back all that money, now.'

I said nothing. I remembered when my own father had died. My mother had lost all his money on horses.

'I'm going out for a walk,' Ginnie said. 'You'll find me at the stables, if you want me.'

I looked at Oliver Knowles' accounts. I had worked out his loan very carefully. I had thought he was going to make eight million pounds in five years.

'Bad isn't it?' Oliver said.

'There's only one hope,' I said. 'You must have the horse thoroughly tested by vets. If there's nothing wrong with Sandcastle, there must be another explanation.'

'Do you think the horse was poisoned?' Oliver asked. 'It is possible. But I know when a horse is sick. Sandcastle has always been very well.'

We had forgotten about Ginnie. There was a loud knock on the door. Oliver answered it. One of the stable lads was outside. I heard Oliver shout – 'She's where?!' Then Oliver ran back into the room. 'Quick, Ginnie's been hurt!'

We ran outside and followed the stable lad. He led us past the stables, to the road at the end of the small field.

Ginnie was lying on her back, by the road. She was trying to say something, '. . . Dad . . .'

'I'm here, Ginnie,' Oliver said, kneeling down on the ground beside her. He looked up at me. 'Get an ambulance, quickly.'

I ran back to the house and phoned for an ambulance.

A man's voice said, 'An ambulance will be with you in ten minutes.'

I ran back to the road. Oliver was holding Ginnie. 'Oh God, what can have happened to her?' he said.

47

'Get an ambulance, quickly.'

The ambulance arrived in ten minutes. Two ambulance-men lifted Ginnie into the ambulance. They drove away. Oliver ran to get his car and we followed the ambulance to the hospital.

A doctor came and examined Ginnie.

'I'm sorry,' he said. 'She died about fifteen minutes ago.'

'She can't have died!' Oliver shouted. 'She was talking to me. She can't be dead! She was talking to me before they took her into the ambulance. She was talking to me!'

'I'm very sorry,' the doctor said. 'She had a very bad head injury. She died in the ambulance. There is nothing we can do.'

A nurse covered Ginnie with a blanket and put a "Do Not Enter" sign on the curtains around the bed. Oliver sat with his dead daughter. I waited outside.

The rest of the night was awful. There were questions to answer and forms to fill in. The police came and asked more questions. A Detective Chief Inspector said, 'It looks like murder.'

Policemen searched the stables and fields as soon as it was daylight. They questioned everyone. 'Who saw the girl last?' 'Where?' 'What time?' 'Did she often go out alone?' 'Was she friendly with any boys – or men?'

I sat with Oliver Knowles while the police searched and asked questions. Neither of us had been to bed. Oliver took a bottle out of his pocket.

'Ginnie was holding this,' he said. 'Why? Should I show it to the police?'

I looked at it. There was a green liquid in the bottle. The label on the bottle said: "Dog Shampoo"[45].

I went to the kitchen and found a small bottle. I poured

some of the green liquid into the small bottle. I would ask Pen Warner to examine it for me. She was a pharmacist. I gave the shampoo bottle to the police.

There was nothing more I could do. I drove back to London, tired and sad. It had been a terrible two days. I wanted to forget about everything that had happened. But again and again I thought about Ginnie and her terrible death.

11

The Third Year: May

Vets were testing Sandcastle. We were waiting for the results. Also, we were waiting to see if any more deformed foals were born.

The bank was waiting to see if it would lose its money. Oliver was waiting to see if he would lose his business. And the police were still looking for Ginnie's murderer.

Oliver phoned me at the end of the month.

'The vets say they can find nothing wrong with Sandcastle,' he said. 'A man wants to buy him. He's coming here tomorrow.'

'What's his name?' I asked.

'His name's Dissdale Smith,' Oliver replied.

'I know Mr Dissdale Smith,' I said. 'I'd like to be there when he comes to see you.'

The next day, I drove to the stables. Dissdale Smith was there already.

'Tim!' Dissdale said. 'What are you doing here?'

'I'm Oliver Knowles' banker,' I replied. 'It was my bank, Ekaterin's, that lent him the money to buy Sandcastle.'

Dissdale Smith looked very surprised.

'Well, you know why I'm here,' Dissdale said. 'If Sandcastle can't be used for breeding, I'm ready to buy him.'

'What are you planning to do with Sandcastle?' asked Oliver.

'I'll run him in races again,' Dissdale replied.

'Or are you going to send Sandcastle to be cured?' I asked. 'That's what you did with Indian Silk, wasn't it?'

'I was lucky with that horse, that's all,' Dissdale said.

'Tell me,' I said, 'is this your idea to buy Sandcastle? Or does the idea come from Calder Jackson?'

Dissdale looked worried.

'It was Calder's idea,' he said. 'But the money is mine. I'll pay twenty-five thousand pounds for Sandcastle. I'm sure no one else wants to buy him, at the moment.'

'Then why do you want to buy him?' I asked.

'Sandcastle saved my life,' Dissdale said. 'I gambled all my money on him once, and he won. He'll win for me again.'

I was very suspicious. I did not believe Dissdale Smith. What was the real reason why he wanted to buy Sandcastle?

I told Oliver to wait and not to accept Dissdale's offer until he heard from me again.

'I'll phone you in a few days,' Dissdale Smith said. 'But don't take too long to decide.'

Then Dissdale got into his car and drove away.

Back in London, I had a phone call from Pen Warner.

'I've analysed[46] your dog shampoo,' she said. 'It's only dog shampoo.'

'Is there anything poisonous in it?' I asked. 'Is there anything that could cause birth deformities in horses?'

'Well, yes, there is,' Pen said. 'If you could get a mare to drink the shampoo, there is poison in it. But horses won't drink shampoo.'

'Of course!' I said. 'You are clever! That's why the vets have found nothing wrong with Sandcastle. We didn't think about the mares. Someone has been poisoning the mares!'

'That's possible,' Pen said. 'There's a chemical in the shampoo called selenium. We know that if sheep eat selenium, it causes birth deformities. Perhaps it can also cause birth deformities in horses. But you would have to get the chemical out of the shampoo and into the horses' food.'

'Can you think how you would get the selenium out of the shampoo?' I asked.

'I'll think about it and call you back,' Pen said.

I had another idea. I phoned Oliver Knowles. 'Oliver,' I said, 'how do you hire your stable lads?'

'When we're busy, I hire anyone who knows the job,' Oliver replied.

'So, would it be possible for one lad to work in many different stables?' I asked.

'Of course,' Oliver said. 'I hire lads for a month or two, then they go off to another stable. They come and go all the time.'

'Thanks,' I said, 'that's what I wanted to know. Have you got a list of all the lads who've worked for you in the past two years?'

'I can find out their names,' Oliver said. 'But why?'

'I'm looking for one lad,' I told Oliver. 'I think this lad has worked at many different stables. He has worked at every stable where a horse has fallen sick and the horse has been sent to Calder Jackson.'

'You're thinking that this lad may have used poison,' said Oliver. 'The problem is that the lad may have used different names.'

'I hadn't thought of that,' I said. 'I'll have to think again.'

Pen phoned. She said that she had found out something about the dog shampoo. I decided to go and visit her in Clapham.

Pen was excited when I arrived.

'I had an idea while I was making coffee and I decided to filter[47] the dog shampoo.'

'And what happened?' I asked.

'I was left with plenty of the poisonous chemical selenium, in my filter. So that's how you get it out of the shampoo. You filter it. I didn't think it was that simple.'

'But how could you get a horse to eat it?' I asked. 'It would still taste and smell of shampoo.'

'You wash away the smell with water,' Pen said. 'Then you put the selenium in something the horse will eat – something with a strong taste.'

'What would that be?' I asked.

'Perhaps linseed oil,' Pen said. 'Linseed oil is sometimes mixed with horses' food.'

'Well done!' I said. 'Now, I have to find someone with bottles of dog shampoo, coffee filters and linseed oil.'

'Who do you think might have those?' Pen asked.

'Calder Jackson,' I said.

'I was filtering the coffee and I decided to filter the dog shampoo.'

'He's going to be on TV tomorrow night,' Pen said. 'It's a live show and he's one of the guests.'

That was all I needed to know. The show was going to be broadcast live. So Calder would be at the TV studios the next evening. He would not be at his house or at the stables in Newmarket.

12

The Third Year: June

The next day, Friday 1st June, I had lunch with directors of a security firm[48]. Ekaterin Bank had lent them a lot of money to make a new burglar alarm. I asked them to help me. I wanted to open locked doors.

They gave me three special keys which could unlock most doors.

'We don't know why you want these keys,' said one of the directors, with a smile. 'If you end up in prison, we don't know you.'

I told Pen Warner what I was going to do. Perhaps I might end up in prison. I told her I was going to look for chemicals or drugs in Calder Jackson's surgery. I said I would show her anything I found.

That evening, I drove to Newmarket and waited until ten o'clock. Calder Jackson was going to be on TV at ten. I was sure that all the stable lads would be watching the TV programme.

Calder Jackson's stables were dark and peaceful. I walked quietly past the house. I could see only one light in the house, in an upstairs window.

My special keys easily unlocked the door marked "Surgery". I went inside, closing the door behind me. There were no windows, so it was safe to switch on the light. I found the light switch, then I began to search the room.

There were labels on all the bottles and boxes of herbs. Calder's pills were in bottles with no labels, but the pills were all different colours.

I took two pills from each bottle and put them in a plastic bag. Then I searched the drawers of the cupboard. There were bags of herbs and packets of seeds, but there was no dog shampoo.

I came to the last drawer. It was bigger than the others. It was full of herbs and plastic packets – nothing else.

I pulled the drawer all the way out, to search in the back. I pulled the drawer too hard and it fell on the floor with a crash! It was much heavier than I expected.

I started to put the packets of herbs back, then I saw there were two parts to the drawer. A black, leather case was hidden at the bottom. I pulled it out. It was heavy.

When I opened it, I saw a name written in gold letters on the inside of the lid:

Ian A Pargetter
Veterinary Surgeon
Newmarket, Suffolk

Ian Pargetter was the vet who had been murdered. His case of drugs and instruments had been stolen. I had found the murderer!

The door opened suddenly. I looked round and saw that the murderer had found *me*.

'Calder!' I said, in surprise. 'I thought you were at the TV studios!'

Calder Jackson saw the vet's case in my hand. He jumped across the room and hit me hard on the head. I fell down. Everything went black.

When I opened my eyes, I was lying on my back in some straw. I was in a horse's stable. A large, brown horse was standing over me. My head hurt.

I stood up, slowly and painfully. There was a small window in the stable. There were bars across it. I looked outside. It was dark, but I could see a light and someone moving.

The light came from the surgery. Calder Jackson was taking things out of the surgery and putting them in his car.

The top half of the stable door opened. I tried to get past the horse, to get to the door.

'Don't try to get out, Tim,' Calder said, 'or I'll hit you again.'

'You murdered Ian Pargetter, didn't you?' I said.

'You know a lot, Tim,' Calder said. 'I might as well tell you the rest. It won't matter, now.'

What did he mean, I wondered – '*It won't matter now.*'

'Yes,' Calder said. 'I killed Ian Pargetter.'

'Why? Because he wouldn't give you drugs?' I asked.

'No,' Calder said. 'He wouldn't give more drugs to the horses he was looking after.'

'So that's how it was done,' I said. 'Ian Pargetter made the horses sick and you cured them.'

'Yes,' Calder said. 'Though I didn't cure them. I simply stopped giving them the drugs that made them sick.'

57

'So, all those stories about herbs weren't true!' I said, in amazement.

'Yes,' Calder agreed. 'My problem was how to give drugs to horses after Ian died.'

'The stable lad!' I said.

'Very good, Tim,' Calder said. 'You should have been a detective.' He smiled. 'My stable lad, Jason, worked for a lot of people. One of the people he worked for was Oliver Knowles.'

'Now, nobody wants that wonderful horse, Sandcastle,' Calder went on. 'So I will have Sandcastle and that fool, Dissdale Smith, will buy him for me.'

'So there's nothing wrong with Sandcastle,' I said. 'Your stable lad poisoned the mares. But why did you use shampoo?'

'Simple,' Calder said. 'If someone found a stable lad with drugs, they would call the police. Nobody thinks that bottles of shampoo are dangerous. I showed Jason how to get the chemical out of the shampoo. He never kept more than two or three bottles at a time.'

'And so you had to bring bottles of shampoo to Knowles' stables, at night?' I asked.

'Yes, and that silly girl, Ginnie, found us one night, in the stables. I had to kill her too, unfortunately,' Calder said.

I was so angry that I tried to push past the horse to get at Calder. But Calder smiled and fed an apple to the horse.

'Goodbye, Tim,' he said. He turned off the light and closed the top door. I was locked up in the dark. I heard Calder drive away in his car.

The horse ate the apple noisily. Then it started to make strange noises and move from side to side. There was not enough room for the two of us in the stable. I was pushed against the wall and fell over.

The horse began to stamp its feet and kick. Suddenly, it went completely mad and jumped and kicked wildly.

Drugs, I thought. He's given the horse drugs to make it mad! He wants the horse to kill me!

I tried to escape to one side of the stable, but there was no room. The horse kicked me in the leg and I felt a terrible pain. I knew my leg was broken.

The horse's hooves hit the wall above my head. Again and again the horse kicked. I knew that if one of those hooves hit me on the head, I would be killed.

Then the horse reared wildly on its back legs. It hit its head on the roof with a terrible smash and fell down onto me. It was dead, but I could not move.

I lay there for hours under the dead horse. It was getting light when I heard the sound of a car.

I thought it was Calder Jackson. He was coming back to find a terrible 'accident' – me, dead in the stables. And how sorry he would pretend to be! What story would he tell the police?

Then I heard a voice call, 'Tim! Where are you?'

I knew the voice. 'Here!' I called back weakly. 'I'm in the stable. Help!'

The stable door opened. Gordon stood there. Judith and Pen were behind him.

'Get an ambulance,' I said. 'And get someone to lift this horse off me.'

Judith ran to find a telephone.

'How did you find me?' I asked.

'Pen told us what you were planning to do,' Gordon said. 'We sat down to watch Calder Jackson on TV. But the programme was cancelled[49] at the last moment. We didn't

The horse reared wildly on its back legs.

know what to do. We phoned Pen, then we decided to come out here to see if you were all right. We found your car outside. Where's Calder?'

'I don't know,' I said. 'But I think he'll be here soon.'

An ambulance arrived. And some men came to pull the horse out of the stable.

The ambulancemen carried me outside. As they were putting me into the ambulance, a car drove up. It was Calder Jackson.

Calder looked at me. He saw that I was alive. Then he saw Pen. She was holding the plastic bag of pills that I had taken from the Surgery. Calder got into his car and drove away at high speed.

––––––

I don't remember anything of the first two days in hospital. When I finally woke up, I was covered in plaster. I had a broken arm . . . a broken shoulder . . . a broken leg . . . broken ribs – everything in my body seemed to be broken! But I was alive!

Two policemen were sitting beside my bed. They were waiting for me to tell them my story. And I did. I told them everything I knew about Calder Jackson – and about the stable lad – Jason.

'Don't worry,' they told me. 'We'll soon find Jackson and Jason.'

They found Calder Jackson in his car. It was parked behind some bushes. He was dead. Calder Jackson had killed himself.

Jason was found many miles away. He was working in some stables in the north of England. When he was arrested, he told the police everything.

Jason explained how Calder Jackson was able to cure sick horses. Jackson got drugs from Ian Pargetter. The drugs were used to make the horses sick. Jackson gave the drugs to Jason. One of the drugs was in bottles of dog shampoo.

It was easy for Jason to get a job as a stable lad. He was good at the work. Jason gave the drugs to the horses, to make them sick.

Then, when the owners of the horses took them to Calder Jackson, it was easy for him to cure them. He stopped giving the poisons to the horses and so they got better!

Jackson had killed Pargetter because Pargetter had refused to give Jackson any more drugs. Pargetter knew that he was doing wrong. But it was too late – Jackson killed him.

And Ginnie had seen Jackson giving Jason the bottles of dog shampoo. She knew that there must be poison in the shampoo. Jason was using the selenium in the shampoo to make the mares give birth to deformed foals.

But Jackson had seen Ginnie watching them. Ginnie had tried to run away, but Jackson had run after her and killed her. However, Jackson did not know that Ginnie had picked up a bottle of the dog shampoo.

So it was Ginnie who had led us to the truth.

13

The Third Year: October

I had to stay in hospital for two weeks. My shoulder and one arm were badly injured and my left leg was broken in many places. The doctors said I would not be able to walk for at least two months. I had to move about in a wheelchair for two months. When I got out of the wheelchair, I had to use a stick. It was a long time before I was able to walk properly.

Oliver Knowles was back in business. His stables were successful again. Sandcastle was fit and well. Everyone knew how the mares had been poisoned by Calder Jackson.

But Oliver would never be a really happy man again. He had lost Ginnie. But he knew that it was Ginnie who had saved the stables.

The bank – or, rather, its Board of Directors – was happy. Their five million pounds was safe.

Gordon and Judith were happy. But Gordon was still a sick man. He was going to retire. Gordon and Judith were going away together, for a long holiday in Australia.

I was not happy. I had to say goodbye to Judith and we saw each other for the last time at Gordon's retirement party. We found it difficult to talk.

'Where are you going?' I asked. I could not think of anything to say.

'Oh, to places we've never been before . . . the Middle East . . . then India . . . Singapore . . . Australia,' Judith said.

It was hard to say goodbye. We were both afraid that we would never see each other again.

. . . we saw each other for the last time at Gordon's
retirement party.

LIVERPOOL HOPE UNIVERSITY COLLEGE

14

The Third Year: December

For the first time in my life, I felt alone and very lonely. I had nowhere to go for Christmas.

On Christmas Eve the phone rang. It was Judith. The phone line was bad and I could not hear her voice clearly.

'Tim,' she said, 'Gordon is very ill. I'm alone and I don't know what to do.'

'Where are you?' I asked.

'We're in Delhi . . . Gordon's in hospital . . . I think he's dying . . . I don't know what to do . . . I need help.' She was crying.

'I'll come at once,' I said.

I packed a suitcase and went to the airport. I arrived in Delhi on the day after Christmas. Gordon had died before I reached her.

———

POINTS
FOR
UNDERSTANDING

Points for Understanding

1

1 Who was Tim Ekaterin's great-grandfather? What was the name of the bank he started?
2 What kind of man was Tim's father?
3 How did Tim's mother lose all their money?
4 Why did Tim work harder than anyone else in the bank?
5 How does a merchant bank make its profit?
6 Gordon Michaels stood in the fountain.
   (a) Who was Gordon Michaels?
   (b) What was strange about him?
7 What was the matter with Gordon Michaels?
8 Who did the chairman want to look after Gordon Michaels' department?
9 What was Tim afraid of doing?
10 'So I asked the artist to come and see me at the office.'
   (a) What kind of films did the artist make?
   (b) Why did Tim want to see him?

2

1 Where did Gordon invite Tim to join them as his guest?
2 Who did Tim want to meet again?
3 How much did the artist want to borrow?
4 Why had Tim not said 'no' to the artist?
5 What is Royal Ascot?
6 Why did Tim wish he had met Judith before she married Gordon?
7 Calder Jackson cured sick horses.
   (a) Was Calder Jackson a vet or a doctor?
   (b) How did he cure sick horses?
   (c) Did Tim believe Calder Jackson?
8 Why was Calder Jackson going to bet on Sandcastle?
9 How much had Dissdale bet on Sandcastle?
10 Which horse won the race? Did Dissdale look happy?
11 I noticed a boy who was watching us.
   (a) How old was the boy?
   (b) What did the boy suddenly do?

12 Why did the police not try to catch the boy?
13 Why did Tim's photograph appear in the newspapers?

3

1 Why did Tim speak to Gordon about the loan to the artist?
2 The phone rang. It was the artist.
    (a) Why did the artist want to increase his loan?
    (b) Was Tim ready to lend him more money?
    (c) Why did Tim decide to lend him more money?
3 We heard that Uncle Freddie was in the building.
    (a) Who was Uncle Freddie?
    (b) Why did Uncle Freddie congratulate Tim?

4

1 Which horse did Oliver Knowles want to buy?
2 How much did Oliver Knowles want to borrow?
3 When does a horse-breeder expect to make a profit?
4 Where were Oliver Knowles' stables?
5 How much money would Oliver Knowles have to make in five years?
6 Why did Tim feel sorry for Ginnie?

5

1 Why was the loan to Oliver Knowles reported in the newspapers?
2 Who invited Tim to stay with them for Christmas?
3 'All my medicines are natural,' said Calder Jackson.
    (a) Where did Calder Jackson's medicines come from?
    (b) What kind of medicines did he never use?
4 Where had Tim met Dissdale before?
5 What kind of work did Ian Pargetter do?
6 Why did Tim remember that Sunday lunch?
7 What kind of work did Pen Warner do?
8 Did Pen Warner believe that Calder Jackson could cure horses by touching them?
9 Why was it difficult for Tim to stay with Gordon Michaels?

6

1 Who did the newspapers say had murdered Ian Pargetter?
2 What had been stolen from Ian Pargetter's house?
3 Who took Sandcastle out for some exercise?
4 How did Sandcastle escape?
5 How did Ginnie try to catch Sandcastle?
6 How did Tim stop Sandcastle?

7

1 Tim invited Calder Jackson to dinner in a well-known restaurant.
    (a) Why was Tim embarrassed?
    (b) Was Calder Jackson embarrassed?
    (c) What did Calder Jackson talk about?
2 Who did Tim invite out on Easter Monday?
3 Where did Tim take his guests?
4 Why did Pen Warner not want Calder Jackson to know that she was a pharmacist?
5 Pen Warner picked up a pill from the floor in Calder Jackson's surgery.
    (a) What was the pill?
    (b) Was it a herbal medicine?
    (c) Could anyone buy this pill in a chemist's shop?
6 'Anyway, it won't happen again,' said Ginnie.
    (a) What would not happen again?
    (b) Why not?
7 How do we know that Tim was in love with Judith Michaels?

8

1 Had the police caught the person who murdered Ian Pargetter?
2 'My dad thought Indian Silk was a champion.'
    (a) What had happened to Indian Silk?
    (b) Who cured Indian Silk?
    (c) Who had bought Indian Silk from Ricky Barnet's father?
3 Why did Tim not tell anyone about Ricky Barnet?

1 Gordon invited Tim to his house for lunch. Who else was there?
2 Why was Tim suspicious of Dissdale?
3 Why were Oliver Knowles' stables quiet?
4 How many foals did they expect to be born in the spring?
5 What was Ginnie going to do when she left school?

10

1 Who would pay for Sandcastle if the horse was sick or died?
2 What was wrong with Sandcastle's foals?
3 Why would the insurance company not have to pay any money to Oliver Knowles?
4 'But what could be the problem?' Oliver Knowles asked.
   (a) How did Oliver Knowles look after his horses?
   (b) What did Tim think might be the trouble?
5 'Quick, Ginnie's been hurt!' shouted Oliver Knowles. What had happened to Ginnie?
6 There was a green liquid in the bottle.
   (a) Where had Oliver Knowles found the bottle?
   (b) What was written on the label?
   (c) Why did Tim pour some of the green liquid into a small bottle?
7 Why had it been a terrible two days for Tim?

11

1 Could the vets find anything wrong with Sandcastle?
2 Dissdale wanted to buy Sandcastle.
   (a) Whose idea was it?
   (b) What did Dissdale say he was going to do with Sandcastle?
   (c) Did Tim believe Dissdale?
3 What chemical did Pen Warner find in the dog shampoo? Was it poisonous?
4 Why did Tim want Oliver Knowles to give him a list of all the stable lads who had worked for him in the past two years?
5 How did Pen Warner get the selenium out of the dog shampoo?
6 How would you get a horse to eat the selenium?

7 Why would Calder Jackson not be at home or at his stables the next evening? What do you think Tim is going to do?

12

1 What was Tim going to look for in Calder Jackson's surgery?
2 What did Tim find hidden at the bottom of a drawer?
3 Who suddenly came into the surgery?
4 Where did Tim find himself when he opened his eyes?
5 Why did Calder Jackson kill Ian Pargetter?
6 Who gave Sandcastle the selenium?
7 Why was Ginnie murdered?
8 What did the horse do after it ate the apple? Why?
9 How did the horse die?
10 Why had Gordon, Judith and Pen Warner come to look for Tim?
11 What did Calder Jackson do when he saw that Tim was still alive?
12 How did Calder Jackson die?
13 Jason told the police everything.
   (a) How had Calder Jackson and Jason worked together?
   (b) How had Ginnie led them to the truth?

13

1 Oliver Knowles was back in business, but he would never be a happy man again. Why not?
2 Why was Gordon going to retire? Where were Gordon and Judith going to go?
3 Why was Tim not a happy man?

14

1 Judith phoned Tim on Christmas Eve.
   (a) Where was Judith?
   (b) Why was she phoning Tim?
2 What happened before Tim reached Judith?

GLOSSARY

Glossary

1 **earn** (page 6)
to get money by doing a job.
2 **drink** – *to die of drink* (page 6)
Tim's father drank so much alcohol that in the end he became ill and died.
3 **gambler** (page 6)
many people *gamble* – bet money – on horse-racing. If you pay money to bet on a horse and the horse wins the race, you win your bet. You get more money back than you paid. If the horse loses the race, you lose all your money. Tim's mother lost all her money betting on horses.
4 **bank** – *chairman of the bank* (page 7)
the chairman of a bank is the chief person in the bank.
5 **files** – *studied the files* (page 9)
all the letters, papers and reports about one piece of business are kept together in a file – a cardboard cover. To study the files is to read through these letters, papers and reports.
6 **loans** – *request for loans* (page 9)
to request a loan is to ask a bank to lend you money.
7 **cartoon films** (page 9)
a cartoon film is a film made with drawings. Cartoon films are amusing and make you laugh. Many cartoons are made using drawings of funny animals – for example, the Mickey Mouse cartoons.
8 **Ascot** (page 10)
horse-racing is very popular in England and there are many famous racecourses, where races are held every year. Special races are held at Ascot every June. It is known as Royal Ascot because the Queen and other members of the Royal Family always come to see the races there. Other famous racecourses are Newmarket, Newbury and Cheltenham. The Cheltenham Gold Cup is a well-known race held at Cheltenham every year.
9 **top hat** (page 11)
a tall hat, covered in silk, worn by men. (See illustration on pages 14–15.)

10 **box** – *special box* (page 12)
    at every important racecourse, there are special rooms called boxes, where friends can sit together. The people in the box can sit at a table and have a drink and a meal.
11 **put a bet on** (page 12)
    to put a bet on a horse is to bet money on that horse, hoping that it will win the race.
12 **cure** (page 12)
    Calder Jackson gives sick horses medicine and makes them better. He cures the horses.
13 **vet** (page 12)
    an animal doctor. The full name for a vet is a veterinary surgeon.
14 **track** (page 13)
    the track is a long, round path at a racecourse, with fences on both sides. The horses run the races on the track.
15 **commentator** (page 13)
    while the horses are running a race, the commentator says what is happening and which horse is winning the race. The commentator's voice is broadcast over loudspeakers, so that everyone can hear him.
16 **reporters** – *newspaper reporters* (page 16)
    Calder Jackson is well-known. The newspaper reporters want to know what has happened to him, so that they can write reports for their newspapers.
17 **hire** (page 18)
    to pay someone to do a job.
18 **loan** – *increase a loan* (page 18)
    to increase a loan is to make the loan bigger by borrowing more money.
19 **studio** (page 18)
    the room or building where an artist works.
20 **relief** – *with relief* (page 19)
    when you think you are going to hear bad news and you hear good news, you are very pleased. The way you speak shows that you are pleased. You speak with relief.
21 **retired** (page 19)
    a person *retires* from work when he/she becomes old.

22 **director** (page 19)

the directors of a bank are the important people in charge of the bank. To be on the Board is to be a director. The Board of Directors meet together to make important decisions.

23 **breeder** – *horse-breeder* (page 20)

a stallion is a male horse and a mare is a female horse. The mare is brought to the stallion, so that she becomes pregnant and gives birth to foals – young horses. A horse-breeder owns stables where he keeps champion stallions – stallions which have won a number of important races. Horse owners pay a lot of money to bring their mares to the stallions. The horse owners hope that when the foals are born, they will grow up to become champion racehorses.

24 **look into it for us** (page 20)

to look into something is to find out all about it. The chairman wants Tim to find out everything about horse-breeding. Then Tim will make a report for the Board of Directors. In his report, Tim will say whether or not it is safe to lend money to someone who wants to buy a racehorse.

25 **worked out the details** (page 21)

Tim has to study and write down all the facts about lending five million pounds. He has to work out – calculate – how long it will take the racehorse-breeder to pay back the money and the interest.

26 **lift** – *Thanks for the lift* (page 24)

to give someone a lift is to take them somewhere in a car. Ginnie is thanking Tim for taking her to her school in his car.

27 **Newmarket** (page 25)

See Glossary no. 8. Newmarket is one of the most famous racecourses in England. There are many stables near Newmarket, where racehorses are trained and bred.

28 **drug store** (page 25)

Calder Jackson keeps the medicines he gives to sick horses in a special room, called a drug store.

29 **fees** (page 26)

money paid to doctors or vets for the work they do.

30 **pharmacist** (page 26)

a person who has studied how to make medicines and drugs.

31 **headcollar** (page 29)

a headcollar is put round the head of a horse. Jason is able to hold onto Sandcastle by fixing a rope to the headcollar which is round Sandcastle's head.

32 **no sign of** (page 30)
when you look for something and cannot see it anywhere, you see no sign of it.

33 **offer** – *pretend to offer* (page 31)
Ginnie wants Sandcastle to come near her, so that she can catch him. She holds out her hand to make Sandcastle think she is giving him a carrot. But she does not have a carrot in her hand – she is pretending to offer Sandcastle a carrot.

34 **embarrassed** (page 33)
you are embarrassed when you think other people are watching what you are doing, or listening to what you are saying.

35 **warfarin** (page 36)
warfarin is a powerful drug. When someone has a heart attack, their heart becomes weak and may stop working. A doctor may give them warfarin to make their heart beat more strongly.

36 **suspicious** (page 43)
you become suspicious of someone when you think that perhaps they are doing something wrong or against the law. Tim is beginning to think that Dissdale is not an honest person.

37 **insured** (page 44)
Oliver Knowles pays money, every year, to an insurance company. The insurance company promises to pay Oliver Knowles a lot of money if Sandcastle has an accident or becomes sick. The insurance policy is a paper from the insurance company on which it says when the company will pay money and how much money they will pay.

38 **deformed** (page 44)
a person or an animal is born deformed if there is something wrong with its body. For example, one of the foals from Sandcastle was born with only half a foot.

39 **ruined** (page 45)
to be ruined is to lose all your money.

40 **poisoning** (page 45)
if a person or an animal eats or drinks poison, they become very sick and perhaps die. They die of poisoning.

41 **vets** – *tested by vets* (page 45)
See Glossary no. 13. Oliver Knowles will have to take Sandcastle to vets. The vets will give the horse medical tests to try to find out why it is breeding deformed foals.

42 *recommended* (page 46)
Tim had made a report on lending money to Oliver Knowles. In his report, Tim had said that it was safe for the bank to lend the money – he had recommended the loan.

43 *accounts* (page 46)
in a business, someone has to write down all the money that comes into the business and all the money that is spent. These figures are the accounts.

44 *destroyed* (page 46)
to destroy an animal is to kill it because there is something wrong with it.

45 *shampoo* (page 49)
shampoo is a special kind of soap, used for washing hair. Shampoo is liquid and is kept in bottles. Dog shampoo is used for washing a dog's hair.

46 *analyse* (page 52)
you analyse something by finding out exactly what it is made of.

47 *filter* (page 53)
to run a liquid through special paper. The liquid runs through the paper and the paper stops anything which is solid. When you filter coffee, the liquid coffee runs through and the coffee grounds stay in the filter paper.

48 *security firm* (page 55)
a security firm is a company which makes buildings and offices safe against burglars. A *burglar alarm* is a device which makes a loud noise when someone tries to break into a building.

49 *cancelled* (page 59)
when something is arranged and then it is decided not to do it, it is cancelled.

INTERMEDIATE LEVEL

Shane *by Jack Schaefer*
Old Mali and the Boy *by D. R. Sherman*
Bristol Murder *by Philip Prowse*
Tales of Goha *by Leslie Caplan*
The Smuggler *by Piers Plowright*
The Pearl *by John Steinbeck*
Things Fall Apart *by Chinua Achebe*
The Woman Who Disappeared *by Philip Prowse*
The Moon is Down *by John Steinbeck*
A Town Like Alice *by Nevil Shute*
The Queen of Death *by John Milne*
Walkabout *by James Vance Marshall*
Meet Me in Istanbul *by Richard Chisholm*
The Great Gatsby *by F. Scott Fitzgerald*
The Space Invaders *by Geoffrey Matthews*
My Cousin Rachel *by Daphne du Maurier*
I'm the King of the Castle *by Susan Hill*
Dracula *by Bram Stoker*
The Sign of Four *by Sir Arthur Conan Doyle*
The Speckled Band and Other Stories *by Sir Arthur Conan Doyle*
The Eye of the Tiger *by Wilbur Smith*
The Queen of Spades and Other Stories *by Aleksandr Pushkin*
The Diamond Hunters *by Wilbur Smith*
When Rain Clouds Gather *by Bessie Head*
Banker *by Dick Francis*
No Longer at Ease *by Chinua Achebe*
The Franchise Affair *by Josephine Tey*
The Case of the Lonely Lady *by John Milne*

For further information on the full selection of
Readers at all five levels in the series, please refer
to the Heinemann Guided Readers catalogue.

199103

Heinemann English Language Teaching
A division of Heinemann Publishers (Oxford) Ltd
Halley Court, Jordan Hill, Oxford OX2

OXFORD MADRID ATHENS
PAULO CH
SING
JOHAN

ISBN 0 435 27218 7

© Dick Francis 1982
First published by Michael Joseph 1982
This retold version for Heinemann Guided Readers
© Stephen Colbourn 1989, 1992
This version first published 1989
Reprinted once
This edition published 1992

All rights reserved; no part of this publication may be
reproduced, stored in a retrieval system, or transmitted, in any
form or by any means, electronic, mechanical, photocopying,
recording or otherwise, without the prior written permission of
the Publishers.

Illustrated by David Eddington
Typography by Adrian Hodgkins
Cover by Chris Burke and Threefold Design
Typeset in 11/13.5 pt Goudy
by Joshua Associates Ltd, Oxford
Printed and bound in Malta by Interprint Limited

95 96 97 10 9 8 7 6 5 4 3